THE GORLESTON [illegible] LIFEBOATS

"ELIZABETH SIMPSON"

S.B. DANIELS

DEDICATION

This small book is written in unashamed pride in being an Honorary Freeman of my home town; a boat-builder, and on the odd occasion a lifeboatman; and it is a tribute to the designers and builders of the famous 'Norfolk and Suffolk' lifeboats which were once the mainstay of the East Coast Lifeboat Service, both Independent and Institution.

Coupled with this must be the un-named hundreds who manned those boats and the womenfolk who endured equal hardship and greater worry; and all too often were left the tragic task of bringing up their fatherless children.

To these, mostly unsung, heroes of the past
and our own heroine of a lifeboat, this book is dedicated.

Stephen Brewster Daniels
Gorleston on Sea, July 1989

THE GORLESTON VOLUNTEER LIFEBOAT 'ELIZABETH SIMPSON'

A LIFEBOAT DISASTER

There can be no conclusion to an argument as to which was the finest lifeboat ever built. Some would say the first because it started the lifeboat saga, but around the East Anglian coastline there can only be one answer – *Elizabeth Simpson*. History abounds with tales of wreckers and cruelties to shipwrecked sailors but deals much less with the tradition of lifesaving which existed long before the term 'Lifeboat' was first used. After all, the saint of lifeboatmen, Grace Darling, made her name in a Northumberland coble, not a lifeboat. Thus it was along our coasts; the beachmen put off in their racing yawls primarily to get a 'huvell', but they brought back survivors as often as they could. Legend attempts to contradict this with the tale of the Gorleston 'Jew Killers' but I believe this yarn, which apparently originated in Australia, was put about by a seeker of either publicity or financial gain and fuelled by pure envy of those who couldn't share in the profits of an exceptionally good salvage job. Certainly there is not one whit of real evidence to support the scandal, and in any event, how could those relatively unsophisticated boatmen have evaded the attentions of the law already alerted by widespread rumour? Still, it is a good tale, dating back to well before 1826.

This photo of the "Elizabeth Simpson" returning from sea gives the opportunity to see some of the rigging. (Photo: Brian Ollington).

The *Elizabeth Simpson* saga starts on 10th November 1888 with the ageing lifeboat *Refuge* going to aid the SS *Akaba* which after grounding on Hammond Knoll, and being refloated by local tugs, had no steering working, so was towed to Winterton and there anchored. She was laden with raw jute for Dundee and due to the very heavy swell the lifeboat was damaged – and her rudder smashed – when going alongside.

Knowing there was nothing his craft could do and with an injured crewman aboard, the Cox'n decided to get a tow home leaving most of his men aboard the steamer with other tugs, and another Gorleston lifeboat standing by. All went well except that on the way one of the twin tow ropes parted and both were bent together giving an extra long hawser.

Approaching Gorleston piers *Refuge* signalled for the tow to be shortened but the Skipper of the tug, misinterpreting the signal, gave the order for the tow to be cast off. The disabled lifeboat was swept onto the north beach and there capsized. Despite heroic efforts by coastguards who were standing by, only three could be saved from the pounding surf. Amongst the spectators on the South Pier was Miss Elizabeth Simpson Stone, a Norwich lady staying at Gorleston, who straightway determined that the boatmen should have another lifeboat, the very best that could be built.

Very soon afterwards a Norwich solicitor's cheque for £500 was received by the Gorleston Volunteer Lifeboat Association, the donor being anonymous. At once a new lifeboat was ordered from Beeching Bros. of Yarmouth, to be called *The City of Norwich*. Into her all the accumulated knowledge, experience and skill of the Beechings and their staff were to be

"Elizabeth Simpson" and crew at the outset of her working life. This is probably the official photo for her launching on October 23rd 1889. (Photo: Norfolk Museum Service.)

incorporated to produce the finest lifeboat ever built. At 48 feet 8 inches she was the largest ever laid down on the 'Norfolk and Suffolk' non-self-righting principle. On the afternoon of Wednesday October 23rd the new lifeboat, now called *Elizabeth Simpson*, for the donor's name had become known, first kissed the water of the River Yare amidst great ceremony. As she was already fully rigged and ready for sea several 'Gentlemen' embarked and went for a trip to the Cockle lightship. Every part and sail were tried with satisfactory results. Regrettably Miss Stone could not be present so was represented by Mr T A Cobbald, but the following day was able to view her gift when the lifeboat was taken up river to Norwich in tow of the steam tug *Star*. Later the crew were 'royally' entertained by the members of the Bridewell Alley St Andrew's Church.

THE NEW BOAT'S DESIGN

Elizabeth Simpson's design generally followed that of Beeching's other well proven Norfolk and Suffolks; only the very finest well-seasoned English oak was used for her keel, stem, stern post and knees; with clean, straight grained prime American Oak for the planks and copper clenched steamed timbers. Time has proved the quality of both materials and workmanship, for 1989 is her centenary year and she can still pass examination for a passenger licence.

At sea, partially under sail and partially rowed. The stern sprit or outligger is clearly seen. "Norfolk and Suffolk" lifeboats had to be rowed in the standing position. (Photo: S.B. Daniels.)

"Elizabeth Simpson" prepares for sea. "Norfolk and Suffolk" class lifeboats were cumbersome to row and the crew would be anxious to raise the masts and sails as soon as possible. (Photo: S.B. Daniels.)

The principle of this design was that the the lifeboat could become one with the sea in very bad weather. Normally the boat would float on its hull with the internal airtanks filling part only of the interior – the entire bows for'ard of the fore tabernacle and the entire stern aft of the mizzen tabernacle; between these, and their supporting thwartship beams, the airtanks filled the sides of the hull leaving only a three foot wide empty area in the centre; this was the ballast tank, filled by pulling out a number of handled six inch plugs set in the bottom. Once these were drawn the lifeboat would float entirely on its air tanks with the sea flowing freely into and out of the hull; only a very high and steep breaking wave could have turned it over. Under sail the extra weight and draught were hardly noticeable. When the plugs were re-located the boat could be baled and pumped clear.

A few figures to add to the overall dimensions already quoted:

The belt (or padding) was 16 inches wide and 18 inches deep, with 22 valves.

The mean draught when fully equipped and manned was three feet.

The centre water ballast tanks had 16 plugs.

There were 23 internal air tanks.

The spars were fore and mizzen yards with a very long 'outligger'.

The sails were dipping forelug and standing mizzenlug.

The manning crew was 21, rowing seven oars aside.

Estimated carrying capacity from a wreck was 150 persons.

The Gorleston Volunteer Lifeboat Association had nowhere to house their new boat, so after buying an old lifeboat shed from the Storm Company they cleared the site and erected a fine new lifeboat house; one of a row of five side by side; an absolutely unique feature. Double doors, with a postern, gave access onto Riverside Road with full width double doors opening to the River Yare at the east end. A massive iron winch was installed at the top of the steeply sloping floor from the river's edge. The Lifeboat rested on bilge runners and a series of iron rollers so it could gain considerable momentum when the retaining chains were slipped. Along both side walls rows of stout wooden pegs bore the solid cork life-jackets and oilskins hung on racks above each side of the bows ready for the crew to collect as they boarded. The shed also had a watchroom overlooking the river reached by a flight of open steps alongside the 'river' doors.

A LAUNCH

It is impossible to recreate the atmosphere and tension within a lifeboat house at 'launching', the suppressed excitement overlain with routine and quiet determination. There are now very few survivors of the era when lifeboats were entirely under oars and sail, although part of my first practice launch was under canvas; so it's the motorised era with its noise and blue haze of exhaust fumes which must be recalled. You go to bed on a bitter February night with a nor'easterly gale throwing handfuls of hail against the windows, and think 'Heaven help the sailors on a night like this' as you go to sleep. *Always prepared you're awake at the first ring of the phone bell and halfway down the stairs before the operator can twirl his handle a second time.*

"Elizabeth Simpson" launches at low water. The harbout tugs, one of which is seen in the background, often helped the lifeboats out to casualties. (Photo: Poppyland Photos.)

'Secretary here'. 'Coastguard; we've a radio call from a trawler that there's a ship aground on the outside of the Haisboro – do you want to call your lads out?' 'O.K. Thanks. I'll get on to the Cox'n'. As an independent lifeboat we didn't qualify for the maroons to be fired so had to dash around hammering on doors to rouse the crew. First, though, the Cox'n is given 'a bell' so he can start in his neighbourhood; then it's pull on trousers, shirt and thick jersey over pyjamas, followed by long woollen seaboot stockings and three quarter length rubber boots before pedalling away for the mechanic's house and from then on the chain grows as each man calls the next in turn. Once at the shed the Cox'n rings the Coastguard for latest details of the casualty's location. Even as he hangs up the receiver the first engine bursts into life and a faint blue haze shimmers in the glow from the bulbs high above the deck and water gushes from the overflow of the engine coolant tank. As the rest of the men dump their bikes and come tumbling through the door the port engine fires and doubles the noise.

The outer doors are hauled open by their rope tackles and the red launching light over the doorway scintillates onto the small river waves as they sweep up and break on the slipway; the blue exhaust haze vanishes in a whirl of sleet as the fumes are dragged away downwind. Within minutes all is ready and the bowman stands above the stemhead waiting to give the signal to slip the chains.

'Launch!' is shouted from aft; 'Launch' echoes the bowman, and with two hammer blows and a rattle of chains she's free. The keel rollers rumble and the greased ways start a wisp of blue smoke as the boat gathers speed before first the rudder, then the already spinning propellors part the dark waters amidst a shower of spray and *Elizabeth Simpson* takes to her element. She turns, then its 'Full Ahead Both' and she's away down river beyond the warmth of the lights, heading for the roaring maelstrom of the Bar. From now on her only contact with the shore will be by the winking of the morse lamp. In the shed the throb of the engines quickly dies; the riverside doors are closed; the Coastguard 'phoned; the watching, the waiting – and the praying – begins.

A poor quality but rare photo of "Elizabeth Simpson" at sea under full sail, probably on a practice launch. (Photo: S. B. Daniels).

THE FIRST QUARTER CENTURY

After such an auspicious beginning the *Simpson* career should be expected to run smoothly, one rescue succeeding another in those halcyon days of lifeboat work. There were many fine rescues; many more fruitless launches; and seemingly *endless wet, dark nights at sea with cold and fatigue greater enemies than the turbulent waters.*

Those were in the future when the crew gathered in the Gorleston Oddfellows Hall for a dinner after the launching ceremony. It seems most of the town had been invited. A telegram received from Miss Elizabeth Simpson Stone wishing them all a happy evening was read and at once answered that the men were thoroughly enjoying themselves and her health would be drunk at nine o'clock. Few of the crew saw their beds that night for they had to be up early to take the Lifeboat to Norwich.

The new Lifeboat was not long in making a commencement on her illustrous career, for just prior to February 1st 1890 the SS *Vectis* of Teignmouth was in trouble. *Elizabeth Simpson* was launched with a full crew and although continuously swept by heavy seas made her way to the casualty and saved both ship and entire crew. The boat's performance was warmly praised by all aboard her; but this launch does not appear in the record book, only in the Yarmouth newspapers. Not until the sixth service on October 26th 1891 does the record book take up the story, and from then on only intermittently, whilst the first recorded saving of lives is not until the 15th launch on December 29th 1894.

Members of the Elizabeth Simpson crew and of Gorleston RNLI Lifeboat crew on a visit to London in 1905. The "Simpson" men wear the lettered ganseyss.

Feting lifeboat heroes. Members of the Gorleston lifeboat crew, who have done such valiant work in life-saving, seeing the sights of the Metropolis. They are here seen on the steps of the National Gallery.

In 1891 the sad news was received at Gorleston that Miss Elizabeth Simpson Stone had died, knowing that her beautiful Lifeboat was commencing to fulfil her hopes; and in continuance of her faith in the project she left the Lifeboat an endowment of £1000 – the income from which was to be used solely to pay 'launching' money to the crew.

Manning *Elizabeth Simpson* was the responsibility of the Ranger Salvage Company (The Storm Company manned the Institution lifeboats) and the closeness of the crew is seen in a launching list which includes three Bensleys; two Flemmings; three Goochs; three Newsons; two Taylors; two Woods and two Whileys, out of a total of 26 men.

December 29th 1894 was a day of strong nor'westerly gales with frequent, violent snow squalls and an immense swell which ran oily with the tide but steeply breaking on the shoals and against the ebb.

From mid morning the Lifeboat had been standing by a Jersey brig with her sails blown away near Corton Sands, but with fresh canvas set the vessel made safe anchorage and the 25 man crew of *Elizabeth Simpson* returned to their homes just before 3 pm. At 7.30 rockets and alarm guns from two lightships brought them, and three others, out into the stormy North Sea again, fighting their way against gale and tide to the Bell Buoy off Caister. There, on the inner side of Scroby Sands, they found the three-masted Rochester schooner *Emily Smeed* almost in her last moments. Despite the terrible conditions Cox'n Job Woods managed to get the Lifeboat close in to the wreck and the eight man crew were soon safely aboard and on their way swiftly to the shelter of the Gorleston Piers to be welcomed by cheering crowds after what was described as *one of the finest pieces of Lifeboat work ever done on the East Coast*. (This rescue had much in common with *Elizabeth Simpson's* last lifesaving service a few miles further north on February 14th 1938 when, with eight others, Job's grandson, mechanic Charlie Woods, helped to snatch six men and the skipper's wife from the tanker SS *Tartary* only minutes before she blew up.)

A crew photo following the "Tartary" rescue in 1938. Back row: Charlie Woods, Arthur "Coddy" Harris, Billy "Dido" Brown, Jack Whymer, Claude Peacock. Front row: Jack Harris, Harry Woods, Billy Brown, Percy Beavers.

Three days later Job Woods and his men had some unusual excitement. The gales had died down to a strong nor'nor westerly when guns from lightships called out the Lifeboat. In the Pightle, outside Scroby and close to Cross Sand they came up with the French schooner *Rachel* of Freamp in a very sorry state, sails blown away, hatches washed overboard, galley smashed and short of provisions. Naturally Cox'n Woods attempted to come alongside to render assistance but was waved away by the French Captain; as he came round for a second try the Captain emerged from below making threatening gestures with a large revolver. Not wishing to 'taste lead' and being unable to communicate verbally the Lifeboat withdrew, leaving the *Rachel* to drift helplessly to Southwold where she went ashore and was lost.

There was considerable rivalry between the two salvage companies when their lifeboats were at sea although this did not prevent the men going in the 'other' boat when necessary; or when trouble flared between the GVLA and the RNLI, or when one body paid better 'launching money' than the other. This last factor frequently caused *Elizabeth Simpson* to stay in her shed when she should have been launched, for sometimes there were only pence in the Volunteer Associations coffers; and even longshoremen's children need food and clothing. Whilst no man joins a lifeboat crew for gain he must in fairness to his family go in the boat which offers him most in return.

THE "ELIZABETH SIMPSON"
VOLUNTEER LIFEBOAT ASSOCIATION,
GORLESTON-ON-SEA
ESTABLISHED

President

Vice-President

Coxswain

Patrons

Bankers

Norwich Trustees

A letterhead of the Association, including the names of the Norwich Trustees.

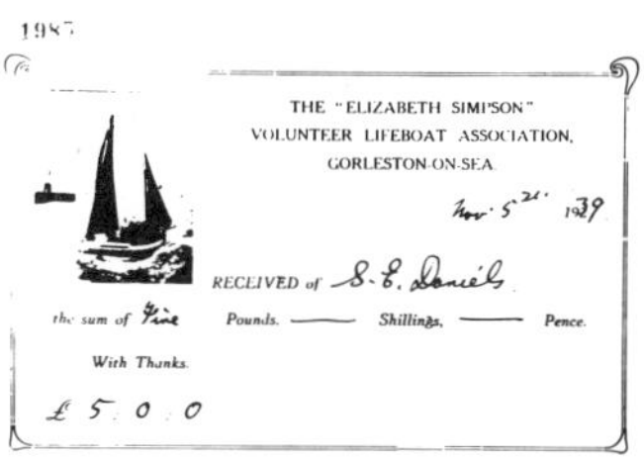
THE "ELIZABETH SIMPSON"
VOLUNTEER LIFEBOAT ASSOCIATION,
GORLESTON-ON-SEA

Nov. 5th 1939

RECEIVED of S. E. Daniels

the sum of Five Pounds. —— Shillings. —— Pence.

With Thanks.

£ 5 0 0

The Association's official receipt.

The maximum payment in *Elizabeth Simpson* was eight shillings (40p) regardless of how many hours – or days – were spent at sea, whatever the conditions; whereas the RNLI paid between ten and 30 shillings (50p – £1.50) according to duration and conditions; although there was more chance of salvage money in the volunteer lifeboat.

FINANCIAL DOLDRUMS

The first two years of the twentieth century heralded just such financial doldrums and not until October 1902 did a change occur when a letter in the press disclosed that a Miss Marter of London had given a donation of £2000 and that henceforth rewards similar to the Institution would be made; these with the unfettered launching procedures should ensure that *Elizabeth Simpson* would be first afloat in times of need and that new energy would be thrown into the concern.

The letter ended with this tribute . . .

'All the Gorleston boatmen are a brave, fearless set of men. Let the gale be ever so furious they never shirk facing the elements if they know the lives of their fellow creatures are in peril.'

By the end of the month the Lifeboat was once more a viable force and went out to two vessels on Trafalgar Day, commencing with a race with the lifeboat *Mark Lane* and culminating in finding the hulk of a capsized lugger .

In all the annals of lifeboat work tribute is very seldom paid to the men of the tugs which frequently towed the lifeboats to the vicinity of a wreck, often in diabolical weather. Most of these tugs at Yarmouth had wooden clencher built hulls and were launched from local yards and fitted with locally built steam engines driving side paddles. By virtue of their overall beam they were very stable in a seaway but pitched abominably. Their crews were every bit as heroic as the lifeboatmen as the following account reveals:

Wrecked Ship. November 18th 1902

'Launched at 11.15 pm in response to guns and rockets from *Cockle* lightship. Wind E. blowing heavy gale. 21 in crew, of whom five were *Mark Lane* men, all under Cox'n 'Crimo' Crisp. 8 hours at sea.

Telephoned to Yarmouth for steam tug, then launched the Lifeboat, the tugs belonging to the Great Yarmouth Steam Tug Company refused to go to sea in such weather but the Nicholson Towage Company sent the *Gleaner* down the river and without hesitation took *Elizabeth Simpson* in (tow). Meanwhile the Royal National Lifeboat Institution boat *Mark Lane* was got ready but the Cox'n could not get a crew for her so was not launched. Our boat proceeded in the teeth of the gale to *Cockle* lightship and found that some vessel had drifted across the bows of the light vessel and the Captain was afraid she would break adrift. No one could be seen or heard a board the wreck which by the time the Lifeboat had arrived was bottom upwards.'

Elizabeth Simpson reached the harbour the next morning at 7.30 am.

This incident, which did not even rank a few words in a local newspaper, hides a tragedy. What was the name of the vessel which fouled the lightship? Where was she from, and bound for? How many widows and orphans did her loss occasion?

In the middle of January 1903 *Elizabeth Simpson* launched three times in 24 hours. One can imagine the pithy remarks of the crew having twice labouriously haled the boat up into the shed *only to send her down the ways again a few hours later*. This sudden surge of activity seems to have been assisted by difficulties between the RNLI and the Storm Company for twice, at least, *Mark Lane* was unable to muster sufficient men.

At 7 am on August 18th 1903 guns from the *St Nicholas* lightship called out the crew who launched the Lifeboat at once and after fighting their way over the Bar against an ebb tide found the schooner *Irish Minstrel* on Scroby. By dint of much hard work in laying out anchors they managed to refloat her at half an hour after noon, thus *saving the vessel and her crew of seven hands*. They reached Gorleston at 2pm.

A number of holiday-makers had an alarming experience when the pleasure boat *Britannia* of Great Yarmouth, with sails split in a squall, was drifting towards Corton Sands that same afternoon. The accident was observed from the high lookout at the Ranger warehouse, the Lifeboat bell rung and *Elizabeth Simpson* quickly prepared for sea again; the smart breeze and strong tide rapidly carried her to the casualty, and knowing that the tug *Tom Perry* was coming up astern as fast as her paddles would drive her, put a rope aboard and stood by checking the drift until the tug got a hawser onto the yawl and towed her in to port. *'Assisted to save passengers and crew to number of 21.'* This is amplified by the local Press:

When the squall hit the *Britannia* the sails split and had to be lowered, so the boat was drifting helplessly until the anchor was dropped. This could find no holding ground and although a small jib was set she continued to drag with the wind and strong flood tide so that the boat got ever nearer to the sands. The situation was getting very serious when *Elizabeth Simpson* came alongside but it was decided not to try to transfer passengers in the choppy sea unless absolutely necessary. The Lifeboat stood by knowing that the tug was hastening to the scene; *it arrived just in time to pull the pleasure boat to safety.*

Schooner *Christean* (200 tons) October 14th 1903

Launched 6.30 pm. Tide Half Ebb, Wind South. 21 in crew; Cox'n G Crisp. 'On Wednesday evening guns were heard from the Cross Sands and St Nicholas lightships. The crew of *Elizabeth Simpson* at once mustered at the boathouse. A message had already been received at Gorleston to tell the Institution boat not to put off as John Burch was just leaving Yarmouth beach. The *Elizabeth Simpson* was however launched and at once made for the wreck. The vessel proved to be the three masted schooner *Christean*, a Swedish craft from Fowey to Leith with a cargo of china clay. She lay on Cross Ridge Sand in about three to four feet of water and great difficulty was experienced by our boat in reaching her ... grounding three times and taking about three hours to wear down to the doomed ship. Three of the crew of the *Christean* were drowned before the arrival of the lifeboat, they having taken to the small boat which was swamped.... *Elizabeth Simpson* returned to the harbour having brought in the three survivors of the crew of six. This was indeed a splendid piece of work, and but for the launching of the *Elizabeth Simpson* we dare not think of the consequences as the Yarmouth boat was unable to reach the ship against the head wind and tide.'

The local press states that *Elizabeth Simpson* was towed out by SS *Burmah* of Hull; but does not mention that the Lifeboat sustained considerable damage to her hull in effecting the rescue. (This was a very clear case of the fallibility of the 'One Lifeboat Only' procedure.)

1904

A testimonial was presented at the White Lion Hotel to Dr Godfrey R Bately on his retirement after 20 years as Honorary Secretary of the Gorleston Volunteer Lifeboat Association. Mr A Whiley eloquently spoke on behalf of the crew before presentation was made of a silver mounted 'Meerschaum' Pipe and a matching tobacco jar. After further complimentary speeches a good evening's entertainment was enjoyed by all.

When *Elizabeth Simpson* was launched to go to the aid of the SS *Cape Wrath* on March 30th the Lifeboat Pennant was flown for the first time from the prominent seamark tower of Gorleston's St Andrew's Church. This white Burgee with a red horizontal centre stripe depicted Elizabeth Simpson in a rough sea coming up to a wreck. Its purpose was to tell Gorleston people that their Lifeboatmen were about an errand of mercy; and they were thus envoked to 'Watch and Pray'. A short verse was composed:

'The Lifeboat is off,
So hoist the Rescue Flag
On Gorleston's ancient shrine of Faith
And Watch and Pray for their return'

(The Pennant is preserved at the Maritime Museum for East Anglia on Great Yarmouth sea front but is in a very fragile condition due to age and many hours flying in strong winds.)

A newspaper report of 2nd August 1904 records *Elizabeth Simpson* had been on the slip at Beeching Bros Yard for repairs to her bottom and sides, sustained in rescuing the survivors from the Christean.

August 4th. This was the first 'Lifeboat Sunday' Service held at St Andrew's by Rev Forbes Phillips. Very much a local character he wrote under the pen name of Atholl Forbes and by marrying into the Cadbury family began Gorleston's long association with the famous chocolate family, further strengthened when Flight Sub Lieutenant (later Major) Egbert Cadbury was stationed at the Yarmouth Royal Naval Air Station, from which he shot down Zeppelin L70 in 1918.

On October 6th 1904 *Elizabeth Simpson* launched to a ketch dragging her anchors and after considerable difficulty, as she was light and drew only a few more inches than the Lifeboat, *managed to save the crew of four and their dog*.

60 HOURS AT SEA

Thursday January 19th 1905 brought a strong nor'easterly breeze and just before 1 pm guns were heard from the lightships. *Elizabeth Simpson* launched with 21 men under 'Crimo' Crisp. (Amongst them, two Childs, three Leggetts, two Newsons, two Taylors and three Woods). Aided by the ebb tide and the tug *Meteor* they soon came up with the 2800 tons, four-masted steel barque *Optima* of Bremen on Haisboro Sands. At first conditions were tolerable so an attempt was made to save the ship by jettisoning cargo and stores. On two occasions when the weather worsened in the next two days the crew had to be taken into the Lifeboats, and later put back aboard. By Saturday evening, with great seas rolling over her, the ship began to break up and *Elizabeth Simpson* tried to wear down to her on a cable from the steam lifeboat *James Stevens* to save the crew. Repeatedly she was carried with great force against *Optima's* side, receiving considerable damage. All night they struggled to rescue the 32 men, managing to take the last ones off just after daybreak. Sail was at once made for the shelter of Yarmouth Roads where some of the men were transferred to RNLI Lifeboats *Mark Lane* and *James Stevens*, although this comradely act was not mentioned in the newspapers.

They were 60 hours at sea. Two and an half long, wet, cold, dangerous days and nights and even those who have tasted the sea in its worse moods must find it hard to appreciate the privations and suffering of the men in *Elizabeth Simpson* and *Mark Lane*; both open boats with no shelter from the elements.

These were real heroes brooking no comparison with today's tabloid celebrities. Hereabouts January nor'easters are known as 'lazy winds', too lazy to go round you *they go straight through, taking the marrow out of your bones on the way*.

Back to the Haisboro Sands again on March 8th; to the SS *Oveido* and this time *Elizabeth Simpson* and two tugs managed to *save the ship as well as the crew after many hard, dangerous hours*.

Palling and Caister Lifeboats had also put off but none of the RNLI Gorleston boats launched. This was due to a dispute between the crewmen and the Instituion over the pay awarded for attending at the *Optima* in January. Apparently the *Simpson* men received £47 each from the GVLA and the *Mark Lane* and *James Stevens* men felt they were entitled to an equal amount as they'd faced the same dangers and hardships, although this was above the usual RNLI scale of reward.

The flurry of intense activity for *Elizabeth Simpson* petered right out in 1906. The turn of the year from 1905 must have been the marker for something which has not been recorded, for not until 2 years later does another service launch appear. Could it have been another financial crisis leading to a 'No Money – No Launch' situation? Who knows now? Dr Bately had tendered his final resignation in January 1907 and although a new committee was formed there does not appear to have been a new Secretary until August 1908; a series of record entries prior to this suggest a more intimate knowledge of events than some of the later ones, but it appears from the many years of similar hand writing that the present record book was not written up until long after the events chronicled. Possibly an earlier book was damaged and only part of it was readable. This could explain the many launches written up in the press but not the book.

At Gorleston quay after returning from the "Walkure" in 1911. (Photo: Brian Ollington).

The entry for December 1st, 1911 is a classic example:

'Barque *Walkure*; G Crisp Cox'n; Brought in crew. 3 masted ship. Salvage.'

A brief press report says that *Walkure* of Hamburg, 1900 tons, was bound from her home port to Santos with general cargo when she went aground on the Haisboro Sands. Palling and Cromer Lifeboats were on the scene long before *Elizabeth Simpson*.

Nine tugs from London, Hull and Yarmouth worked for three days attempting to free the barque but in vain and when the weather deteriorated and the vessel was in danger of breaking up *Elizabeth Simpson* took off 22 men, then had to go back for the cook and steward; and *brought all 24 into Yarmouth along with a considerable amount of salvaged goods*. The tugs were unable to get alongside the stricken ship.

When called out on 12th August 1912 the Record Book says:

'Steamship *Egyptian* on Scroby Sands. Eventually sank. Lifeboat accepted. Crew saved. Salvage.' Only deep searching may reveal the details.

Christmas 1913 must have been an unhappy time on the Gorleston Quay for after the RNLI Lifeboat had launched to a vessel on 20th December the crew went on strike when they were refused pay as the Caister men, already off in *Covent Garden*, claimed the Gorleston boat had 'trespassed' on their area. How long the strike lasted is not recorded but *Elizabeth Simpson* had no crew difficulties in early 1914 as this gem of an entry shows:

'January 9th 1914. Cox'n G Crisp; 23 in crew. Launched at 8.20 pm. Schooner *Morton Castle* on Cockle Sands; services accepted; saved 3 white men, 21 black men and 7.' (Seven what? Did their colour defy description?)

"Elizabeth Simpson" loaded with bales salvaged from the "Egyptian", 1912. (Photo: S.B. Daniels).

THE SECOND QUARTER CENTURY

The fourth wartime entry only tells part of the story of how *Elizabeth Simpson* eventually found a small boat with five men from the Lowestoft trawler *Compare* in a 'grave position' on Scroby on January 24th 1915. Wartime newspaper publishing restrictions forbad a detailed report.

Lifeboatmen were not in danger only from the elements as July 10th 1916 shows. *Elizabeth Simpson* and the tug *George Jewson* went together to Corton Gat where SS *Karra* had either been torpedoed or mined. The crew had taken to their boats and been picked up by Lowestoft Lifeboat but the two Gorleston craft towed the vessel out of the channel where she broke in halves and sank. *'Great risk was run by the tug and Lifeboat owing to numerous mines about the spot.'*

Then on the 29th, with only 15 men in the crew, Cox'n Crisp launched to a vessel on Haisboro Sands. When they arrived with the tug *Yare* the vessel appeared to have got clear by herself; but then they sighted Submarine *H9* on the Sands and eventually with the assistance of the *Yare*, *Fastnet* and *United Service* freed her from the Sands and into deep water. A footnote adds 'This launch must be kept strictly private at present.' H9 had a crew of 30.

At 10.45 am on February 16th 1919, a tug found her way into the harbour through thick fog and passed word that a steamer was aground on North Scroby. 'Crimo' Crisp launched at once and went out in tow of *United Service*. Two hours later they found the casualty and were engaged, with tugs *Yare*, *George Jewson* and *Despatch* to get the SS *War Valley* off with her valuable cargo of 4000 tons of coal. Despite the flowing tide she remained fast and towing wires and cables broke with damage to *Elizabeth Simpson*; fortunately there were no injuries. All day a heavy sea had been running and a rapid freshening of the easterly wind at nightfall sent the tugs hurrying for shelter – but *Elizabeth Simpson* stood by the wreck all night and at 7.15 am *took off all 37 of the crew*. In the conditions this was a great feat of seamanship and the Lifeboat was eventually forced to cut her cable for safety, thereby losing her anchor. The gallant *George Jewson* had now come out again and towed the Lifeboat back to Gorleston by 9.30. Amongst other damage she'd lost part of her padding and the men declared they'd not had such an experience for the last twenty years. Damage was estimated at £115.5.0.

The SS *Hopelyn* in 1922 was a famous rescue; at the time of the alarm Cox'n Crisp was visiting HMS *Kennett* but mustered his crew when told the Caister Lifeboat was already on the way out, but neither *Elizabeth Simpson* nor RNLB *Kentwell* launched. When it was later learned that the Caister boat could not get off the beach the Harbour Master requisitioned the

George Jewson and instructed her to take out the *Kentwell*. Their efforts were in vain for there were no signs of life on the steamer. The next day RNLI Cox'n Billy Fleming called for a crew and nine *Simpson* men helped ten of his men to take the *Kentwell* out again, and this time saw signals from men on the wreck but could not get near her. Returning to port the Lowestoft Motor Lifeboat *Agnes Cross* was met. Cox'n Fleming made a dangerous leap aboard her and explained how broken steel plates, which couldn't be seen in the dark, were protruding from the vessel. All returned to Gorleston. At 5.30 the next morning with seven Gorleston and ten Lowestoft men aboard the *Agnes Cross* set off again and by virtue of higher water and slightly finer weather had *rescued the 24 men and their black cat* by 9.30 am with great credit to the bravery of all involved, including Cox'n Crisp who received commendation for his services as signalman aboard one of the tugs.

MOTOR POWER

Once again *Elizabeth Simpson* lay unused in her shed, out-dated and made redundant by the new motor lifeboats, from December 1924 to August 1926; when she launched for the last time as a 'pulling and sailing' lifeboat; she then went up river to Newman's the Marine Engineers to have twin Kelvin 30 horse power sleeve valve petrol/paraffin engines installed. The entire centre section of the boat was cleared, engine bearers painstakingly

"Elizabeth Simpson", under motor power, crosses the bar on a Lifeboat Day launch. (Photo: Rick Leggett).

fitted and a watertight steel engine room installed above them, flanked by large capacity fuel tanks. All controls were brought on deck so that the hatch could be closed to prevent water reaching the engines. At the same time a slightly higher deck was fitted over raised airtanks, preserving the buoyancy, but the ballast wells were left intact. When hauled back into her shed she looked magnificent in fresh paint with the shining bronze propellors beneath each quarter. *Hopes were high for a new beginning, but funds were desperately low.*

The following July saw the loss of an old work mate. It was a foggy day and fairly calm when *Elizabeth Simpson* launched to aid a ship on the north end of Scroby. Skipper Stubbs of the drifter *Torbay*, YH 103, had heard her siren and cautiously crept in to see if he could help before going off to alert the *Cockle* lightship. Returning he put a tow rope on to the casualty and tried to hold her from driving further onto the sands. *Elizabeth Simpson* and *Yare* arrived together but whilst the tug was manoeuvering to connect her tow she struck a submerged wreck, believed to be the SS *Hopelyn* and began to sink.

The Lifeboat was quickly alongside and safely took the four man crew off the vessel which had so frequently helped her to attend other shipwrecks. The screw tug *George Jewson* later managed to pull the steamer clear. Caister Lifeboat stood by throughout the operation.

When the Dutch oil tanker *Georgia* was wrecked off Cromer on Monday 20th November 1927 Lifeboats from as far away as Southwold were involved, the main action being centred on the *H F Bailey* and *John and Mary Meiklam*, both RNLI boats. The former, from Cromer, did heroic work in saving 16 of the crew from the stern section whilst the latter from Gorleston made many desperate attempts to get near to the bow section to save the 15 men thought to be still aboard, only to be repeatedly defeated by shallow water and terrific seas, not knowing they'd already been saved by another Dutch vessel.

The superstructure of the "Georgia", taken when the sea had abated and a photographer could safely make the trip to see her. (Photo: H. H. Tansley).

Elizabeth Simpson was delegated a lesser role in this combined operation. Thinking there were still men to be saved special Schermuly lifesaving apparatus was rushed from London in a hired Daimler breaking all speed restrictions at an average of 40 miles per hour. On arrival at Gorleston at half past six Tuesday evening the 12 six pound rockets, each with 350 yards of line, 12 two pounders with 250 yard lines, two pistols, six rope lines and a tripod were loaded onto the broad decks of the Volunteer Lifeboat which at once put to sea heading for Haisboro Sands. Arriving at the wreck in pitch darkness they 'dodged' the long night away watching for any possible signs of life until after daylight when, convinced there was no one left aboard, they returned to harbour to put ashore the Board of Trade officials sent to supervise the use of this most modern equipment; and then must have watched with envy as the gear was unloaded, knowing how wonderful it would be to possess even one item of such equipment.

Just a month later the two Gorleston rivals were again off, to the SS *Oscar* of Helsingborg with her cargo of sawn timber blazing furiously. The ships crew managed to get away in their own boats and were picked up by *John and Mary Meiklam*. *Elizabeth Simpson* had been requisitioned by the Underwriters and with their representatives and Oscar's Captain and Engineer aboard had stood by as *George Jewson* and *Tactful* fought the fire with their monitors. On returning to port they were just about to land the passengers when the maroons were fired and the *Meiklam* went surging past them to a reported casualty. Not a lucky day for the Volunteer boat.

The Gorleston Lifeboat "John and Mary Meiklam" in 1924. Transferred from Cromer, she was a "Norfolk and Suffolk" class vessel, but was motorised from the outset. "Elizabeth Simpson" is moored in the background. (Photo: Poppyland Photos).

From the above reports it is clear that 'lifeboating' was not always strictly lifesaving; March 3rd 1935 classes as a borderline case when *Elizabeth Simpson* went off to the Cockle lightship for a nine hour round trip in very rough seas to bring ashore a member of the crew who'd either been injured or taken ill. An ambulance awaited their return. At the end of June the Lifeboat had a more sombre role.

The close ties with St Andrew's at Norwich had been maintained over the years so on the death of Mr Bottomley, a Naval Architect and brother in law to the Vicar it was natural to turn to *Elizabeth Simpson* to help fulfil his wish for his ashes to be buried at sea. On arrival at Brush Quay the casket and mourners went aboard, the ensign was lowered to half mast and the urn covered with the Union Flag.

After proceeding to midway between *Corton* lightship and the South Scroby Buoy the Lifeboat hove to and the burial service was read by the Norwich vicar. Some of the ashes were scattered on the sea before the Honorary Secretary – Pilot Hayman – got out onto the padding and held the casket under water until it filled and sank. A wreath was left floating on the lonely waters. On return the mourners were taken up river to the Haven Bridge. It seemed fitting that the Lifeboat's engines were 'Kelvins' and Mr Bottomley was nephew to Lord Kelvin.

A NEW REGIME

There now ensued one of the Gorleston Volunteer Lifeboat Association's periodic crises. For some years the Ranger men had converted *Elizabeth Simpson* for passenger carrying during the summer, running sea trips for visitors from Brush Quay, using the slogan 'Help us in summer to save drowning men in winter' An admirable concept which was not being entirely fulfilled as very few lives had actually been saved since the engines were installed in 1926. In many local eyes she had already ceased to be an active service lifeboat and at the end of 1936 all the non-Ranger members of the committee resigned.

In answer to a 'grapevine' appeal two names were submitted for Chairman and Honorary Secretary, Harry Woods and the author of this work respectively. The former, with a bent for marine engines, and the latter a boatbuilder and longshore skiff owner, were both well known to the Company men and accepted without reserve so a new committee could be formed. The new 'brooms' had ideas for a clean sweep, and that summer there was no 'tripping' but the Lifeboat was open for inspection in her shed with a rota of attendants to show visitors round. The former 'tripping' crew suffered some hardship for their summer earnings were no more, but the shed collections exceeded the previous summer's net profit on passengering.

In the summer months of the 1930's, "Elizabeth Simpson" takes on temporary seating, including park benches, for use by "trippers".

Another happy occurence also increased the new awareness of the Lifeboat as well as providing a small addition to the funds. As soon as the date of Coronation Day was announced permission was sought to take *Elizabeth Simpson* to Norwich for the occasion and have her open to public inspection, with postcards and a collection box prominently displayed aboard. Herbert Frazer, the Lord Mayor granted permission and the Norwich trustees enthusiastically supported the plan.

The Guildhall,
Norwich.

15th April, 1937.

Dear Sir,

I have your further letter of the 13th instant with reference to bringing the "Elizabeth Simpson" Lifeboat to Norwich on Coronation Day. Naturally there will be no objection to your making a charge for visiting the Lifeboat or taking a collection on the boat itself but not on the river bank.

As I mentioned in my previous letter, if you still wish to bring the Lifeboat to Norwich please communicate with the Town Clerk so that a berth may be reserved near Foundry Bridge.

Yours very truly,

Lord Mayor.

Mr. S.E.Daniels,
19, Park Road,
Gorleston-on-Sea.

The Lifeboat's association with Norwich continued throughout its working life as this 1937 letter illustrates.

Launching was at 4.30 am on May 15th. It was a calm but very foggy morning; good time was made until we passed under the Breydon railway bridge then it was a matter of feeling the way from channel post to channel post until the Berney Arms public house was reached; by eight o'clock the fog began to clear and the rest of the run was sheer pleasure except for keeping the speed down to prevent too much wash upsetting moored boats and damaging the river banks. Consequently arrival at Foundry Bridge was 30 minutes late. Once moored the reception by the Norwich Trustees was warm and included an invitation for the entire crew to lunch at Mr E Bullard's expense at The Lord Nelson on the opposite side of the River Wensum. All that beautiful day the citizens of Norwich *honoured their Lifeboat* and contributed to its work, so it was very late when the lifeboat shed was reached again.

For many previous years August Bank Holiday Monday had been 'Simpson' Flag Day in Gorleston, but in 1937 the Borough Watch Committee did not grant permission for this to be held. This was a devastating blow to the newly appointed officers; previous occasions had been an important source of revenue ever since the GVLA had been the first lifeboat organisation to commence the practice of an inshore demonstration. Funds were too low to ensure a winter's work.

Cap in hand the officers made an appointment with Yarmouth's formidable Chief Constable – Mr Ben Smith – and so pleaded their cause that he backed them at the next Watch Committee meeting and a very successful Flag Day and demonstration launch was held; even the weather smiled. Things now looked much better until the Cox'n, 2nd Cox'n and mechanic resigned, feeling unable to work within the new committee's guidelines which included allowing non-Company men to make up the crew. Other members of the Ranger Company were more supportive and the positions were filled by Mr Jack Whymer and 'Dido' Brown (both Company men) with Charlie Woods (Job's grandson) going as mechanic and the Chairman (Harry Woods) as his second. For the first time a signalman was listed – and trained in morse and semaphore.

Aboard the boat other changes were made; dynamoes were fitted to both engines and navigation and working lights changed from Colza oil to electric, First Aid equipment was placed aboard, as were emergency rations; regular practice launches instituted with all the equipment being tested; thus allowing training of a number of keen youngsters who now flocked to the lifeboat carrying out maintenance and watching completely voluntarily. Representations were also made to the Coastguards so that the Hon Secretary would be informed of emergencies on equal terms with the RNLI.

The passengers look well-pleased with their excursion as "Elizabeth Simpson" returns to the quayside, probably in 1936. Lifebelts are required to be carried for such trips. (Photo: B. Stone and Son).

"Elizabeth Simpson" returns from a passenger trip. Such excursions earned a little extra revenue for hard-pressed funds. (Photo: Brian Ollington).

These excursionists undoubtedly enjoyed their "trip" as it appears to be a flat-calm day. (Photo: S. B. Daniels).

October 1st saw the first service launch under the new regime, with a crew of four Company men and four newcomers. It was a false alarm but proved that the 'turnout time' needed to be improved. Two more launches before the end of the year proved that *Elizabeth Simpson* was back in business; but had added no 'Lives Saved' to the Records.

'Dido' Brown used to cheer us with the saying *'Every dog has his day'* and that came on February 14th 1938 – St Valentine's Day.

All through Sunday 13th the wind had been slowly freshening from the nor'west, building a very heavy swell right through the Roads and when it went round to nor'east and gained strength during the evening heavy squalls of sleet and snow set in. So it was no great surprise when the Coastguard telephoned in the early hours of Monday to say a trawler had radioed North Foreland reporting that they'd seen a vessel on the outside of Haisboro Sands; the message had been relayed to Gorleston Coastguard who advised both local lifeboat Secretaries as well as Caister and Cromer. Caister considered their chances of getting off the beach very slender but both the *Elizabeth Simpson* and *Meiklam* crews mustered. At the GVLA shed the engines were warmed up and everything made ready whilst Cox'n Whymer on the telephone tried to ascertain the exact position of the casualty – without success – she was lost in a welter of squall and spray somewhere on the southern half of Haisboro. It could be that a similar situation prevailed with the RNLI for neither Cromer nor Gorleston boats decided to launch in the uncertainty as to whose territory the wreck was in. At 4.40 am the Hon Secretary slipped the chains and sent *Elizabeth Simpson* out into the night and after visiting the Coastguard Station and the Mariners Refuge – where fires were already being lit, blankets warmed and kettles set to boil – went to wait by the telephone.

As she cleared the pierheads *Elizabeth Simpson* lost the last of the ebb which had helped her down to the Bar and encountered not only the full force of the biting gale but also a strong flood tide. With engines running full out it took two hours to get abreast of the *Cockle* lightship, anchored where the Haisboro ended. Decision time would be whether to go outside the Sands, where the wreck had last been seen several hours before, or inside. Not knowing the position where she'd originally stranded, or her size, there was no knowing how much water the casualty drew or whether she could have bumped right over the Sands in the raging surf. Tormented eyes strained into the darkness as the Lifeboat slowly fought her way nearer the lightship and then suddenly, just as as they came abreast of the plunging 'Float' one of the crew shouted 'There!' as a red rocket glowed fitfully for a moment; away to the nor'west. At once the helm was swung and their battle with the elements continued on a slightly easier course. Now the seas rolled in from the starboard bow instead of aimost dead ahead. The crew huddled on deck seeking what shelter they could in the lee of the engine casing between taking turns as lookouts. All were now thoroughly chilled in the biting wind and soaking spray which seeped down inside the neck of the oilies; the plugs had been drawn as soon as the broken seas were encountered so now water sloshed deeply around their feet as wave after wave rolled aboard as they neared the shoals.

Their quarry, plainly visible between the squalls as they rose on the waves was barely afloat, drifting helplessly just outside the surf line. Cox'n Jack endeavoured to bring his craft into the casualty's lee so that the men waving from her bridge could jump down into the Lifeboat, but both were yawing wildly in the hob-gob of broken water and at the first attempt *Elizabeth Simpson* was flung hard against the ships side when the propellors, screaming hard astern, cavitated in the plunging motion. No one managed to jump onto the heaving foredeck. Full astern out – come round – and go in again. This time the propellors gripped at the crucial moment, the forward way was checked and half ahead on both held the Lifeboat for a long minute scraping and jarring the damaged padding against the unyielding metal plates, long enough for four bedraggled humans to judge the second, leap and be dragged to safety. Third time lucky going in and three more came aboard; *'That's all of us'* shouted the rescued skipper.

'Full astern both' and *Elizabeth Simpson* clawed away from the threatening hulk. By now the surf was to windward; already they were in deeper water.

The Lifeboat crew huddled round the survivors as the rum bottle was passed around and warmth flowed into their veins from the uplift of spirits at the rescue as well as from the bottle. Heading downwind with the full flood under them the mizzen mast was raised and the ensign hoisted to the truck in triumph as they raced between the dozens of ships anchored in the Roads for shelter, some raising a tattered cheer as they passed at the sight of the ensign and the huddle of figures on the open deck.

The old sea dog had had her day at last. Six men and the Skipper's wife saved only minutes before watchers on the shore suddenly saw the tanker SS *Tartary* blow up and vanish for ever.

Elizabeth Simpson had only one more significant launch; but it was a 'Royal' occasion. For many years before coming to the throne the Duke of York had organised a summer camp at Southwold for young men from the less fortunate walks of life and as King George V1 he continued this practice and on his way to a visit arrived in Yarmouth Roads aboard *Victoria and Albert* on Monday August 1st, then a 'Bank Holiday'. The Royal Yacht was escorted by the destroyer HMS *Boreas* and in the evening a party was sent ashore in her whaler to pick up 'The Royal Mail'. They failed to return at the expected hour and finally the alarm was raised. Maroons were fired and both lifeboats launched at 3.50 am on Tuesday. It was then high water so the first of the ebb bore both boats swiftly to the two vessels anchored off Britannia Pier. *Elizabeth Simpson* started to come alongside *Victoria and Albert* to be greeted by 'Don't make a noise. Mind the paintwork' in stage whispers, before being guided in by hand signals. They were then ordered to report to HMS *Boreas* to take a naval party ashore to help pull up her whaler lying damaged on the beach. But, as they pulled away, a couple of the lads swore they saw the faces of two young Princesses peering at them from a window. On arrival at HMS *Boreas* they learned that the missing whaler had been recovered and there were no casualties so their services would not be required.

Apparently the boat's crew had missed the steps at the end of the pier and then found the surf on the beach too much for them.

Buckingham Palace sent a memorable letter of thanks.

Elizabeth Simpson spent most of the next six months undergoing a complete overhaul, the first since engines were installed in 1926, and to repair damage sustained during the SS *Tartary* rescue. The outbreak of war in September 1939 brought her service career to an end and saw the younger members of her crew dispersed, some never to return. All through those long years she lay in the shed, unused and almost forgotten; not even in the crisis of Dunkirk was she brought into service, a terrible shame as her shallow draft and immense carrying capacity could well have been very valuable there.

THE LAST HALF CENTURY

For many peace in Europe did not bring the end of the War, nor did the total surrender of Japan; another full year elapsed before the remainder of *Elizabeth Simpson* crew counted their depleted ranks and the cost of the years of neglect to their well-loved lady. She would never be a lifeboat again; perhaps it was as well, after all **50 years of honourable duty without losing a man of her crew, or a guest, must be well on the way to establishing a lifeboat record**; especially when the other figures are taken into account. In the record book are *121 Service launches to 125 vessels, plus 12 before the First World War* which were reported in the local press but for reasons already conjectured never entered in the book. The total number of lives she helped to save will probably never be accurately assessed; there are too many entries like 'saved crew' without quoting a figure, and newspapers in the 19th century did not make large detailed features of lifeboat work; it was too commonplace on this coast. *The undisputed quoted figure is 441, but the real total cannot help but be well over 500*. Three 'youngsters', George Mobbs, Paul Williment and Percy Beavers, who helped make up her crew in the middle and late 1930s, became Cox'ns in the RNLI lifeboats at Gorleston after the War, which speaks volumes for their dedication to lifeboat work and the opportunity they received when the 'Company' manning system was relaxed.

Amongst this "tripping" crew are George Mobbs, Dollar Leggett and William Halfnight. (Photo: Brian Ollington).

In February 1946 the now elderly remaining members of the Gorleston Salvage Company – formerly 'The Rangers' – wound up their organisation and a whole slice of maritime history in lifesaving and salvage began quietly to disappear. Harry (Dollar) Leggett, Secretary of the Company since 1921, had been a staunch supporter of the Lifeboat; had participated in and then witnessed the end of the pulling and sailing boats; had helped man the new motor lifeboats; seen the revoluntionary wartime airborne lifeboats come into Gorleston and before his death watched the yellow Air Sea Rescue helicopters fly out over the waters he'd known so well. This was the end of an era, just as the War had brought an end to the 'longshoreman' and his way of life.

A Public Notice appeared in April 1948:

> GORLESTON-on-SEA. The Gorleston Volunteer Lifeboat Shed, also the Volunteer Lifeboat known as Elizabeth Simpson. Sale by auction, May 12th at 11 am on premises. Auctioneers A V George and Co Ltd.

The shed went for £400 but the Lifeboat only made £90. She was bought by Mr B C Norton, newly returned from naval service, who at first intended a conversion to a holiday cruiser but then decided to try 'passengering' with her. Naturally the powerful Kelvin engines would not be necessary and many alterations had to be made to equip her for the new work, so she was sent to Herbert Woods Broads-Haven Yard to have two new Morris Commodores fitted and the other alterations done. The craft which came back down the river looked a very different one; she floated higher in the water and the familiar pillar box red 'padding' had been replaced with a wide red rubbing strake beneath the blue sheer strakes. A raised 'bridge' had been built amidships over the engine room from whence was controlled the steering quadrant fitted to replace the former aft worm drive wheel fitting. The beautiful lines of her hull were now even more obvious. Mr Norton purposed to use her for passenger work and fishing trips on and out of the River Yare, and the Board of Trade granted a 'Passenger Certificate' for her to carry 80 persons. For a few years she worked from 'The Bend' at Gorleston, and is remembered as having two Cox'ns – Ted Harris and his Collie dog – but a couple of seasons of moderate business through constant sou'easterly winds added to high running and maintenance costs forced a move the following season to calmer waters up river from Lowestoft swing bridge. Initially this was a very successful move but as costs continued to soar the decision to part with her had to be made.

Mr W V Beale had returned from engineering work at various mines in India and taken a seasonal job aboard an ex Fairmile – *The Golden Galleon* – which ran trips from Yarmouth Haven Bridge; when he heard that *Elizabeth Simpson* was for sale his heart was lost and he put every penny of his cash into her purchase. 1956 was his first season with her, working from the North Quay, making some trips to sea and some up river. Following alterations to the 'bridge' and seating the Board of Trade granted a new licence for 76 passengers at sea or 90 up the Yare or Waveney. Unfortunately there was too much competition at the Yarmouth site so two years later the scene of operations was moved to Lowestoft Harbour for similar two directional voyages but when difficulties arose over the use of Mutford Lock her berth was moved to Oulton Broad, with passengers brought from Lowestoft by motor coach for the run through

Oulton Dyke to Burgh St Peter and other places on the River Waveney. In 1963, during this period, she was again re-engined, this time with a pair of Perkins diesels. Skipper Beale had the same respect for *Elizabeth Simpson* as had her pre-war crews, and he lavished every care on her but increasing years and failing health, ascerbated by the Mutford Lock difficulties and expenses led him to reluctantly part with 'The Lady' at the end of the 1976 season. For twenty years she'd been his life, but by the middle of the following February she bore his ashes for scattering on Breydon Water.

Two views of "Elizabeth Simpson" on Oulton Broad when owned and skippered by Captain Beale. Her wide rubbing strake has gone and a simple cover offers shelter to her passengers.

Two views of "Elizabeth Simpson" on the river at Potter Heigham. Amongst the crew are Sam and Alf Cook; the photos probably date from 1950. (Photos: Sam Cook).

Some boats are more fortunate than others; usually its called 'luck' but old time builders reckoned there was more to it than that.

They believed part of the spirits of those who conceived, built and ran a vessel were absorbed into her structure and that from them she acquired a spirit of her own; therefore a boat which was happily built and loved throughout its life gave it all back. How else can it be, as her subsequent crews avowed, that she always dipped her bows. whatever the tide, wind or weather, as she passed that place on Breydon where the ashes of a man who loved her as much as had her 'life-saving' crews were cast onto the tide.

Just prior to Skipper Beale's retirement she was bought by Pleasure Steamers of Great Yarmouth and the following summer once more came back to her berth just above the Haven Bridge from whence passengers were taken for trips across Breydon and up either the Yare or Waveney rivers; with varying success according to the seasons. In 1985 she was bought by the Pennant Group, successors to Herbert Woods Ltd. at Broads-Haven, and operating from her usual berth the following year took visitors both up river, as previously, and down past her old Shed to the Bend, to see the wealth of shipping using the port and its specialised North

Sea oil and gas facilities. Now, after another re-engining with BMC 3.5 Commodores, and a re-fit she works from the Pennant Yard at Potter Heigham, down the River Thurne to St Benet's Abbey and Ranworth; *still working at 99 years old, and looking forward to her Centenary*. Veritably a grand old lady.

Now all that remains of the days of glory, apart from the altered hull itself, are the Record Book, one only of the six record boards which used to grace the south wall of the shed, many photographs, a couple of models, the burgee (or Pennant), and one of the Great Yarmouth coats of arms which used to adorn her bows; mostly in the keeping of the Maritime Museum for East Anglia on the seafront at Great Yarmouth; but owing to their condition neither the record book nor the burgee are on display. There must be other mementoes about; hopefully some will come to light to augment this unique collection. What the future holds for this wonderful craft is uncertain but the Friends of the Maritime Museum are hoping she will not go the sad way of so many of the famous old lifeboats but remain in the port which saw her conception and construction, as a fitting tribute to all those who go down to the sea in ships *specifically to help others in distress*.

In a tangible way her spirit and tradition carries on for the Caister Lifeboat, at the other end of the Borough, is also independently run – the great work goes on; heaven forbid that the Caister Volunteer Rescue Service is ever so handicapped, nay almost crippled, by lack of funds as was *Elizabeth Simpson*.

Surviving members of the 1930's crew of "Elizabeth Simpson" received the Honorary Freedom of the Borough of Great Yarmouth in 1984. (Photo: Ivan Gould).